I0035960

The Truth About Network Marketing Revealed by Nkuli Mkhize

ISBN 978-1-928155-25-6 (Softcover)

Table of Contents

ACKNOWLEDGEMENTS

It's amazing how quickly you can get anything done once you make a decision. The writing of this book is testimony to that. The primary motivation for the writing of this book is the deep need within me to empower others. I have been empowered and I believe in the principle of passing it forward. In my interactions while building my network marketing business, I identified the need for aspiring entrepreneurs, as well as people seeking financial freedom in general, to be educated about the powerful business model of network marketing.

The Company that is my partner for my network marketing business is the first to be acknowledged. I thank its founders, it's executives and it's top income earners for inspiring me to empower others by sharing with them our company and this amazing business model. I thank them for empowering me as a person, which in turn makes me a better businessperson and an asset to society.

Secondly, I would like to acknowledge and thank **Raymond Aaron and his 10-10-10 Program** for enabling me to write this book so quickly. With the inspiration from my network marketing company, and the foolproof guidance of the 10-10-10 Program, I was able to complete my book in 3 months. I would not have been able to realise this dream without either of these enablers, who whom I owe my gratitude forever more.

I would also like to acknowledge my team members, **Team Mteule, Team Achievers and Team Cousins**, for encouraging me and believing in me. Their unwavering support has been invaluable on this journey.

Sharon Cousins and Simone Solarsh, I would like to acknowledge you for being my second eyes before this book went for publishing. I really appreciate your input.

Last but not least, I would like to thank my family; my parents **Nombulelo and Armstrong Qwele**, you guys are my rock. Thank you for believing in me, always.

To my husband **Sibusiso Mkhize**, thank you for always allowing me to shine, to be all I can be, and your inspiration to help me achieve; and to my boys, **Zasembo and Yamambo,** for sacrificing their time with me and allowing Mommy to finish this project. You guys are my WHY and I love you unwaveringly.

FOREWORD

"A book like this is extremely relevant at a time when traditional businesses are shedding more jobs than creating them, globally; when more and more middle class people are faced with the reality of not being able to maintain their lifestyle if they choose to retire at retirement age; when the world is faced with crisis after crisis, financial meltdowns, recessions, you name it.

The middle class now needs, more than ever, options to assist them to get out of the crisis of not being able to make ends meet, even though they did everything "according to the book." They went to school, found good jobs, and were supposed to have been set for life; the painful reality they face is that they are not set for life. So they go and get more degrees, and the more degrees they get, the more debt they incur, and the more things don't change, or get worse. The reality is that if one is not progressing, they are unfortunately not maintaining, they are regressing. The stark reality facing the middle class is that the majority live from hand to mouth, with more and more debt acquired to maintain their lifestyle, and no solution in sight. Many companies are no longer able to guarantee jobs, especially at Senior Management and Executive Levels, most jobs are now fixed term contracts as opposed to permanent, so there are no longer any guarantees; this is sadly trickling down to even more junior positions.

Those who happen to be doing well financially, either as a result of being in a high paying executive position, in a specialized job, or owning their own business, unfortunately have to sacrifice all or most of their time in order to maintain their jobs and their financial freedom; but is that freedom? Are the sacrifices worth it? Is being too busy to watch their kids grow up a worthy sacrifice?

However, the beauty of the Network Marketing business model is that it is an equalizer. It is not only accessible to those who have plenty capital or access to capital. The truth is, the majority of the world is unable to access capital to start businesses because they more often than not do not have the necessary collateral required by banks or even Development Finance Institutions these days, to secure loans for the businesses.

This book is dedicated to the masses that need a level playing field; who do not want to let their past or present determine their future; who want to get out of the shackles of poverty and help others do the same. This book is dedicated to TIME & FINANCIAL FREEDOM SEEKERS from all walks of life, globally. It is intended to bring back belief in people that THEY CAN, whether they are working class people who have always lived a life of struggle, middle class people unable to make ends meet, or financially well off folks, but time broke; all

4

of us can achieve a life of TIME & FINANCIAL FREEDOM. At the end of this book, you will know EXACTLY how to move forward if you want to move towards TIME & FINANCIAL FREEDOM.

This book and the Network Marketing business model, however, IS NOT INTENDED for those who are not decisive about what they want, it's not for people who are looking for a hobby— it's for people looking for a business that is going to take them to their goal of TIME & FINANCIAL FREEDOM." **Raymond Aaron – Best Selling Author of Double Your Income Doing What You Love, Canada**

1

MY PEOPLE PERISH DUE TO LACK OF KNOWLEDGE

Someone once told me that the meaning of POOR is the Passing Over of Opportunities Repeatedly.

I'm certain that we have all passed up opportunities because we were too lazy to wake up, too lazy to do something out of our ordinary routine; too lazy to investigate further, and too comfortable in our comfy zones.

More often than not, we pass up opportunities because we don't give ourselves time to thoroughly investigate those that come our way due to what we've heard in the past about bad experiences either in that industry, investment opportunity, or business model.

But do we ever investigate these new opportunities for ourselves? Do we give ourselves a chance to compare fact versus fiction, or fact versus opinion?

Do we give ourselves a chance to actually see what those opinions are based on, and then decide for ourselves if they make sense? Have you ever heard the term "a dog does not bark at a stationary car?"

Do you realise that anything progressive in this world will have critics? People fear the unknown, but you can't pass up an opportunity based on another person's uninformed opinion of what may or may not work for you.

You owe it to yourself to do due diligence and to satisfy yourself on the actual facts.

This book is intended to help you with the majority of that due diligence exercise. Your job of finding a vehicle to take you to your TIME and FINANCIAL FREEDOM goal should be an easy one once you have finished reading this book.

TIME & MONEY POVERTY

What would you do if you could afford to work - a fraction of the time you are currently working - for yourself, instead of someone else? How would you spend your new-found free time? What are the things you would do that you desire but can't do now because you simply don't have time to do? Travel? Charity? Spend time with your kids? The reason why you should ask yourself questions upfront is because your answers will determine the kind of vehicle you want to take you to your future goals.

This book is for people who are truly seeking TIME and FINANCIAL FREEDOM. People who want to make a mark on the lives of those around them, and people who want to leave a legacy behind for their children and their children's children.

What if I told you that this is possible for EVERYONE? You just need to know the vehicle(s).

I'm a firm believer that we were all created equal. With or without the right connections, whether or not you were born on the right side of the highway, legitimately earned TIME and FINANCIAL FREEDOM is attainable by all of us. And get this, you don't need a bank loan; you don't need to use your house, your car, or your mother-in-law to secure the funding; the barriers to entry are extremely low too. Stick with me and I'll show you how.

Some of you don't necessarily have financial constraints, but the high cost of your financial well being to your health and your family may be detrimental. You may just need the freedom of time, but because you sell your time for money, it's a catch 22 situation.

You may think you will no longer have financial freedom when you leave your source of income (job or business), well stick with me and I'll show you how you can achieve TIME FREEDOM without sacrificing your FINANCIAL FREEDOM. It is never advisable though for you to leave your job/current business until you have managed to replace your income (preferably more than 1 time) with the PASSIVE INCOME you make from your new business. One of my mentors, Loral Langemeier, calls this new business/vehicle a Cash Machine. As much as this business should in time free up your time, it should give you time income on a frequent basis (daily or weekly).

Loral has put together a **120-Day Plan To Quit Your Job** that she makes available only to her clients. She charges these clients thousands of dollars to get access to this and many other tools, but she has agreed to make this bonus available FOR FREE to you, my dear reader, and you can access this bonus now at www.TheTruthAboutNetworkMarketingRevealed.com/bonuses.

COMMON CHARACTERISTICS OF THE WEALTHY

I'm going to make an assumption here that the reason you are reading this book is because you are interested in TIME and FINANCIAL FREEDOM. I'm going to make the assumption that this book was not forced down your throat and that you are reading it of your own free will. So I'm going to be frank in this book.

In my interactions with wealthy people—as mentors, colleagues, business partners, etc.—, there are a few distinct traits I have observed about them. I have been taught, am experiencing and am convinced that creating wealth is not difficult; it's about finding people who have already achieved what you want to achieve, and model yourself after them in order to have the kind of success they have achieved. Now modelling means copying, so you need to spend time with these people, listen to them, read about them, whatever is possible in order to learn their behavior, their habits, how they talk, how they treat people, and how they approach life. The biggest advantage about modelling is that those you are modelling have gone through the path you want to take and can show you how to avoid the painful lessons that they have had to endure, making your journey easier, faster and far less painful.

Open Minded

One of the most common characteristics of wealthy people is that they are the most open-minded people I have ever met, over and above other traits, such as being solutions oriented, problem solvers, and genuinely interested in serving others. Most wealthy people do not pass over opportunities without first educating themselves about them. They then make an informed decision to either take advantage of the opportunity, or let it go.

Money comes easily and in abundance

The world of making money is two-fold; one is about working hard and sacrificing time, health, and family in order to maintain it. The other one is about working smart, working less, and leveraging other people's efforts, ethically, while at the same time empowering them and helping them achieve their FINANCIAL and TIME FREEDOM goals to maintain it. Which one is most appealing to you?

Many coaches and mentors in this journey of wealth creation have taught me that one of the key formulas to wealth creation is to surround yourself with those who have accomplished their goals and have become successful. You will be surprised at how willing most of these people are to share their success formulas with you; you will be surprised by their absolute humility and their sense of duty to empower others, it is so powerful it rubs off.

One of the most fundamental things taught by these millionaires and billionaires is that money comes easily. In fact, the more money you make, the more you make money.

- o   Step 1 is to believe that MONEY COMES EASILY.
- o   Step 2 is to believe that YOU DESERVE IT.
- o   Step 3 is to DECIDE that you are going to MAKE THE MONEY without breaking your value system. You'll be amazed at how Providence just moves in your favor once you make a DECISION.
- o   Step 4 is to change your mindset about any negative beliefs you have about money, it is NEVER ABOUT RESOURCES; it is ABOUT RESOURCEFULNESS. You have to divorce yourself from saying, "I can't afford it" to "How can I afford it?" You would be amazed at what your mind comes up with once you tell it a different truth. Tell your mind that YOU CAN'T AFFORD NOT TO, and watch as possibilities and opportunities open up for you.

- o Step 5 is to look for a vehicle that is going to get you there, one that makes the most sense to you.
- o Step 6 is to set clear goals (make them big) with regards to your TIME, FINANCES and LIFESTYLE, then work backwards to determine what you need to do on a daily, weekly, monthly and annual basis in order to achieve your goals.

With regards to making your goals big, the following story will give you a sense of what I mean by BIG. We were recently honoured by a visit from Les Brown (one of the most renowned motivational speakers in the world and popular author) at one of our company training sessions and when closing, he told us to put down our FINANCIAL FREEDOM NUMBER. Then he told us to multiply it by 100. That's how ridiculously BIG your goal needs to be.

Setting goals and achieving them are a vital part of success. But this is not a goal-setting book, so I won't go into more detail on how to set or achieve goals. However, my mentor and friend Raymond Aaron has written a bestselling hardcover book entitled, **Double Your Income Doing What You Love**. He is recognized as the world's #1 authority on goal achievement. In fact, on the back cover there are testimonials from giant celebrities who use his program. One such testimonial is by Jack Canfield, the co-creator of the Chicken Soup For The Soul series. Here is his testimonial: "The reason I personally choose to use this amazing system for myself and for my company is that, bluntly stated, it is the most powerful system ever created." By special arrangement I have permission to allow you, my dear reader, to own a copy of Mr. Aaron's book for FREE and you can get an instant download by simply going to: www.TheTruthAboutNetworkMarketingRevealed.com/bonuses.

I know the two FREE bonuses discussed above will add tremendous value to your journey of wealth creation, I know this because they have done the same for me. There will be more FREE bonuses to take advantage of later in the book and because they are on a first come first served basis, it is in your interest to read the book as quickly as possible in order to get to them.

Coming back to our discussion of spending time with accomplished individuals in order to learn from them; the problem is that when you are not in the circles or networks discussed above, you are not exposed to the different wealth creation vehicles. I'm about to reveal to you one of the most powerful vehicles, which is often misunderstood by those not involved in it, and therefore miss the incredible opportunity it brings; and that vehicle is Network Marketing; Robert Kiyosaki (International Best Selling Author of *Rich Dad* books and games) calls it the Business of the 21st Century. In this book, we will discuss some of the fatal flaws of some of the features of this business model, but will also reveal how in time, these have been resolved by some companies in the industry, in order to ensure that the industry delivers on it's core attraction, that of being an equal opportunity provider.

CONCLUSION

9

The intention of this chapter was to get you thinking about your life, about your dreams and aspirations, about your belief systems and your values, before we delve deeper into the vehicle that is network marketing.

What this chapter is also trying to impress upon you is that, as much as everything in life begins with the acquisition of knowledge, anything meaningful is preceded by a Decision, followed by Action. It does not matter how much knowledge you acquire, through whatever means; it does not matter how many seminars you attend, it makes no difference in your life until you DO something about the knowledge. Knowledge IS NOT power, but ACTING ON THAT KNOWLEDGE is power. Action is, however, preceded by a DECISION; then there is context to the ACTION. You cannot act on all the information you consume; it is only information related to the path you have DECIDED to follow that will be of most use to you. That is why it is critical that you go now to www.TheTruthAboutNetworkMarketingRevealed.com/bonuses in order to claim the two bonuses discussed in this chapter.

It is my wish that as you read this book, it helps you make the necessary DECISION about the path you are going to follow once you have finished reading the book, and resolve to ACT on that decision. In the words of Eric Worre, the Network Marketing Pro, "It is my wish ladies and gentleman that you DECIDE to be a Network Marketing Entrepreneur, because it is a stone-hard fact that it is the Better Way." This book will reveal to you why Eric (and I) believe this to be the truth. I'm looking forward to this journey with you.

2

WHAT IS NETWORK MARKETING

Before I go into deeper discussions about why Network Marketing is the Better Way, I need to make sure we are on the same page with regards to our understanding of what Network Marketing is or is not.

Network Marketing is one of the most misunderstood business models in the world today. One reason for this is because it seems too good to be true, and many who try it do not make a success of it. It is an amazing business model indeed, when you compare it with a job or traditional business, but it's definitely not too good to be true when you educate yourself about it and realize that it's very logical how Network Marketing Entrepreneurs make money. You will also realize that the business model is not perfect. There are flaws in some of the elements of its makeup, but newer companies using this business model are using their past experience to perfect the model, so that the flaws don't take away from the sheer supremacy of the business model.

DEFINITION OF NETWORK MARKETING

According to Wikipedia, Network Marketing is a marketing strategy in which the sales force is remunerated for personal and team sales. These salespeople are responsible for selling products directly to consumers, and for building a team of other salespeople to do the same. By doing so, they are compensated not only for the sales they make, but also for the sales the rest of the salespeople in their teams make; resulting in more than one level of compensation. The compensation does not usually end with direct and override commissions, but is often accompanied by additional bonuses when certain levels of sales and sales team building are achieved. The methodology used in this industry is relationship referrals and word-of-mouth.

So, at its simplest definition, Network Marketing is word-of-mouth marketing. According to Eric Worre, in his book entitled, *GoPro*, Network Marketing is a way to promote products and services to the people who need them. I will dare to add that Network Marketing is a way to promote products and services to the people who need them, *at competitive pricing.*

All companies can choose to use the traditional model of advertising using billboards, newspapers, magazines, or by hiring sales staff, which they have to look after, etc. Or, companies can use Network Marketing methods of relationship referrals and word-of-mouth advertising to market their products to those who need them the most. It is predicted that because of technological advances, which are resulting in many jobs that used to be critical in the past now being irrelevant, Network Marketing will make more sense to companies in the near future and this is why. The current trend globally is that companies are starting to structure remuneration to their employees more and more based on performance. It is predicted that this trend will continue to the extent that companies in the future are expected to pay employees purely on performance. So Network Marketing, which consists of a voluntary sales force, incentivized to build relationships that will ensure repeat and new sales, is starting to make more sense to even traditional companies. We are already seeing a number of traditional companies complementing their traditional marketing with Network Marketing programs (i.e. compensation based on referrals - think of timeshare and property sales referral programs, insurance companies referral programs, etc.).

So the traditional companies using Network Marketing programs, as well as pure Network Marketing companies, provide all the corporate support and pay distributors on a performance basis to promote their products. This has proven to be extremely effective for companies because word-of-mouth advertising seems to be working better than any other form of marketing, with some traditional companies even admitting to how well their Network Marketing Programs are working. The companies then take the money they would have spent on advertising, promotion, and a big sales force with its related support services like Human Resources, and pay it to their distributors to spread the word

THE DIFFERENCE BETWEEN NETWORK MARKETING AND DIRECT SELLING

Some people use Direct Selling as a synonym for Network Marketing. However, according to author Dominique Xardel, Network Marketing, also known as Multi-Level Marketing (MLM), is only one type of Direct Selling.

According to Wikipedia, multi-level marketing has existed since the 1920s and 1930s with companies like *Nutrilite*, or *California Perfume Company*, which was renamed as Avon.

According to Xardel, Direct Selling refers to the distribution system, which is shared by both Direct Selling companies and Network Marketing companies. According to Dr. Charles King, Professor of Marketing at the University of Illinois in Chicago, both Direct Selling companies and Network Marketing companies use word-of-mouth as the medium through which they distribute their product or service. The key difference between these two, however, is the approach. Direct Selling companies are only about "the sale," closing the deal. Network Marketing is about relationship building, nurturing customers, and giving them an opportunity to participate in the sales of the product they use and love. While Direct Selling is a business of products, Network Marketing is a business of people. The Direct Selling Association ("DSA"), a lobbying group for the multi-level marketing industry, reported that in 1990 twenty-five percent of members used MLM, growing to 77.3 percent in 1999. Companies such as Avon, Electrolux, Tupperware, and Kirby all originally used single level marketing (or direct selling methodology) to sell their goods, and later introduced multi-level Compensation Plans. By 2009, 94.2% of members were using MLM, accounting for 99.6% of sellers, and 97.1% of sales. The DSA has approximately 200 members while it is estimated there are over 1,000 firms using multi-level marketing in the United States alone.

HOW DOES IT WORK?

Independent, non-salaried participants, referred to as distributors (or associates, independent business owners, independent agents, business representatives, etc.), are authorized to distribute the company's products or services. They are awarded their own immediate retail profit from customers, plus commission from the company through a multi-level marketing Compensation Plan, which is based upon the volume of products sold through their own sales efforts, as well as that of their downline organization[1].

Independent distributors develop their organizations by either building an active consumer network, which buys directly from the company, or by recruiting a downline of independent distributors who also build a consumer network base; thereby expanding the overall organization.

Additionally, distributors can also earn a profit by retailing products they purchased from the company at a wholesale price.

COMPENSATION/INCOME LEVELS

The financial barriers to entry for Network Marketing are extremely low. This serves as both an advantage and a disadvantage for the industry. The advantage is the fact that anybody, on any budget and any social status, can afford to start a Network Marketing business immediately, or almost immediately. The disadvantage is that anybody can afford to make the investment and even if they don't make their money back or a profit, it's not such a big deal since it was not a large capital investment anyway. So many people join as a hobby and when they realize the business actually needs work in order for it to get to profitability, they give up and often badmouth the company, the product, and the industry, sometimes legitimately, sometimes not. Eric Worre calls these people posers. "They are not serious about building a business; they just want to get involved in something "cool."

1

[1] This term will be explained in Chapter 5

Eric goes on to explain that some of the posers who don't quit immediately graduate to "amateurs" who don't equip themselves with the skills required in the industry and who often deviate from the recommended methodology of running the business. They rely on their own instincts, timing and luck. Sometimes that works for them, but when it does not; they quit and, like the posers, often blame the company, the product, and the industry. Additionally, because they are so desperate, they often damage relationships with friends and family because of their uneducated approach.

Eric goes on to explain further that some of the amateurs, however, realize there must be more to the industry and their respective companies because they find that people they know or have met, are consistently making vast amounts of money with the same products/services, and the same Compensation Plan. They give themselves time to investigate things properly, study these people, their behavior, how they do business, and mimic them, and eventually end up on the same path as these top income earners. In many MLM companies as little as 10% – 25% (on average) of its business associates are making any real money, but 10%-25% are making some serious money. Most MLM companies have Income Disclosure Statements though, which are publicly available and not only give the above mentioned statistics, but also give statistics of actual average income earned at all levels in any given financial year.

You see, like anything in life, everything we do is a choice, and it's on the basis of that choice that we get results; it's the same in Network Marketing. Those who decide to take the Network Marketing opportunity seriously, those who decide to take it as a profession and run it as a business, reap the rewards of doing that, and the rewards are amazing. But those who do not, those who fall in the categories explained above, who happen to be the majority, do not get to experience those benefits and results. So the lesson is, if you are going to take on an experience you have not taken on before, and achieve the results of those who have succeeded in that field, you need to listen to and follow their advice.

You would remember though that some of the quitters have legitimate reasons for quitting, and it boils down to their intention for starting a Network Marketing business. The average person joining a Network Marketing company is not a serious business builder, therefore from their point of view, the amount of work required at the beginning in order to make the business successful, is not really what they signed up for. They signed up for something that is not going to require too much of their time and give them a steady stream of secondary income. These are not the people who are looking to quit their jobs, and therefore they can't afford the time initially required to bring the business to a level where most of the income comes from other people's efforts. So there is a mismatch in their objectives and what is required.

CONCLUSION

14

It is important for you to know your reason behind joining a Network Marketing company or starting a Network Marketing business, because this will determine what kind of company you join and whether its compensation plan is suitable for your needs and goals.

3

WHY NETWORK MARKETING IS NOT A PYRAMID SCHEME

DEFINITION OF A PYRAMID SCHEME

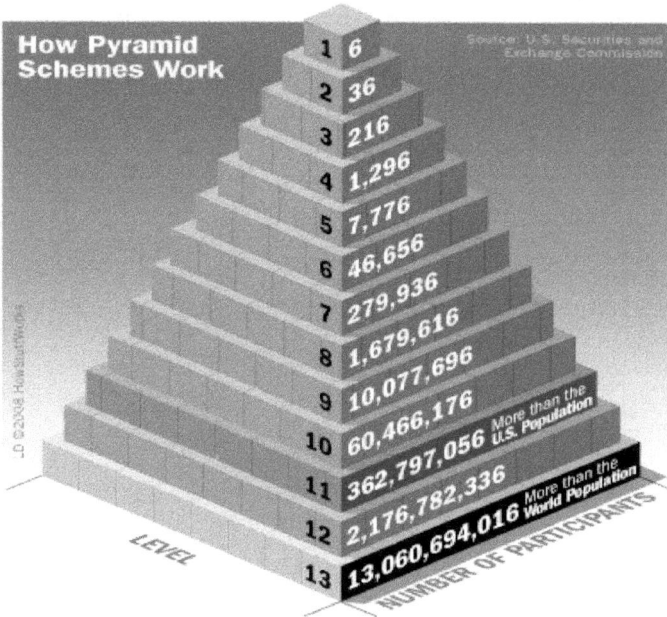

The above diagram shows how a pyramid scheme is unsustainable due to the fact that the number of participants, as per the formula or Compensation Plan of the scheme, will end up exceeding current world population. This is obviously impossible. Not everyone in the world, or even in a country or town will be interested in the same business opportunity, so an assumption that this is the case is a fallacy.

If a company cannot show you its position in its market, industry or sector, and how it's competing with other companies in the same space (regardless of the business model they are using – therefore whether they are using the Network Marketing business model or not) and what its growth trajectory looks like (i.e. is it a Start Up, in the Growth Stage,

16

Expansion Stage or Mature Stage), that's a warning that it may not be a legitimate opportunity.

A successful pyramid scheme combines a fake, yet seemingly credible, business with a simple-to-understand yet sophisticated-sounding money making formula, which is used for profit. The essential idea is that a "con artist," Participant #1, makes one payment, which is the only payment he/she will ever make to the scheme. To start earning, this participant has to recruit others like him who will also make one payment each. *He or she then gets paid all of the money received from his/her recruits.* Then when those recruits go on to recruit others, participant #1 gets a cut from the money those recruits paid to get into the scheme. Therefore as the scheme continues and more and more people are recruited, Participant #1 gets a portion. However, because of the fact that there is no actual product or service exchange, the scheme becomes impossible to sustain because the people involved end up being too many to share the new money coming in. .

To enhance credibility, most such scams are well equipped with fake referrals, testimonials, and information. I have personally found that the best way to allay my fears about opportunities in Network Marketing is to ask for details of the company's head office, as well as the names of the company's executives and top income earners; and do my own investigation on those individuals. If I find they are credible individuals, I get the comfort level I'm looking for.

The flaw in these scams that are mimicking Network Marketing is that there is no end benefit. The money simply travels up the chain. Only Participant #1 and a very few at the top levels of the pyramid make significant amounts of money. As discussed above, due to the fact that there are only so many times you can split a dollar, the amounts earned by later participants decrease sharply down the pyramid slope. In fact, later participants who do not manage to recruit end up with a shortfall. In a real Network Marketing company, a person in the 100th level is able to make as much money (and more) as the person in the 1st level; it's just a matter of time and effort on their part.

Many pyramids are not as simple as the model discussed above. They realize that recruiting many people may be a challenge for most, so they simplify it by requiring each person to recruit two people. But each person recruited has to recruit his or her two people and so on, as illustrated in the diagram below.

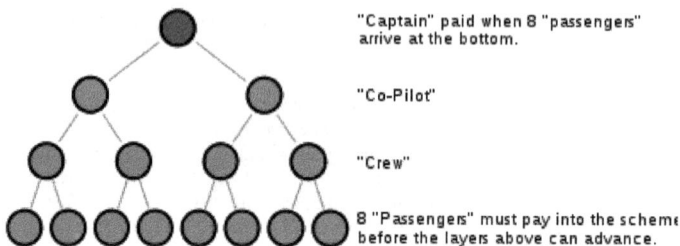

"Captain" paid when 8 "passengers" arrive at the bottom.

"Co-Pilot"

"Crew"

8 "Passengers" must pay into the scheme before the layers above can advance.

These schemes go by different names including, Airplane Game, Original Dinner Party, Treasure Traders, etc. Each game has four tiers as illustrated above with different names denoting seniority. Whatever they are called, the common thread among all of them is that they have a total of 15 participants with Tier 1 (one person), Tier 2 (2 people), Tier 3 (4 people) and Tier 4 (8 people).

The above diagram illustrates The Airplane Game; where, the person at the top is the "captain," (that is Participant #1), the two below are "co-pilots," (Participants 2&3) the four below are "crew," (Participants 4 -7) and the bottom eight are the "passengers." (Participants 8 – 15)

What typically happens is that the last eight participants (i.e. the passengers), have to join the scheme with a pre-determined amount, e.g. ($1,000). The sum of all Tier 4 contributions (a total of $8,000) goes to the "Captain," who must then leave the scheme, with everyone who remains moving up one tier. This would of course result in two Captains (Participants 2&3), which necessitates a split in the group; with each group requiring eight new passengers. These eight participants have to wait until 3 more tiers have been formed beneath them to get a return on their investments. If the group does not grow to that level and the pyramid collapses, they have lost their money.

Someone using this model, as a scam would fill up the first 3 levels of the Airplane with fictitious names, which would make them end up with the payment of the last tier participants without having put down any money, then they would leave and rejoin as a passenger under the real investors and wait for his/her turn to advance to "Captain" again with the passengers' money, making 7 times their investment. This person would continue re-entering the scheme under the real investors each time they "graduate" as Captain and make 7 x their investment until the scheme collapses.

Regardless of whether the scheme is used legitimately or not, it is still an unsustainable and unethical way of making money; therefore it is a pyramid scheme.

There are many other forms of scams out there, but they all have similar characteristics, regardless of how they are structured of what they are called.

The United States Federal Trade Commission warns that it is best not to get involved in plans where the money you make is based **primarily** on the number of distributors you recruit. Preference is to be involved in plans where you make money based on your product sales volumes. It states that research is your best tool. Below are some of the steps they recommend you follow:

1. Find, and study, the company's track record.

2. Learn about the product.

3. Ask questions.

4. Understand any restrictions.

5. Talk to other distributors of the company.

6. Consider using a friend or adviser as a neutral sounding board, or for a gut check (*assuming you're hearing the opportunity from a stranger*).

Many well-known MLM companies have enough accolades from and partnerships with well-known and well-trusted industry bodies and organizations to give them the credibility they require. Additionally, these industry bodies and other organizations are unlikely to recommend or partner with these companies without doing a thorough investigation of their businesses because their reputation would also be at stake. Some of these partner companies are Ernst and Young, Payoneer Mastercard, World Travel Awards Organization, Direct Selling Agency, some Stock Exchanges in the United States, etc. Additionally, the Network Marketing business model is recommended by well-respected individuals like Robert Kiyosaki, Donald Trump and Les Brown, to name but a few. I will discuss these recommendations further in Chapter 7.

CONCLUSION

Credibility is key to determining the genuineness of a Network Marketing opportunity. Credibility is derived from independent sources that have nothing to gain by associating themselves with the said opportunity. This is what separates genuine Network Marketing opportunities from scams.

Additionally, Compensation Plans of genuine Network Marketing companies are carefully and intricately put together by professionals like Actuaries in order to ensure there is a cap in the percentage of revenue paid out to Business Representatives/ Distributors/ Business

19

Associates, which therefore makes the business model and the company sustainable. I would urge you though to still make sure that in your mind, the positioning of the product or service in the market makes sense (e.g. is it relevant, is it competitively priced, etc).

I trust that this chapter has enabled you to comfortably differentiate between a genuine Network Marketing Company and a Pyramid Scheme.

4

THE MECHANICS OF NETWORK MARKETING

INTRODUCTION TO THE NETWORK MARKETING COMPENSATION PLAN

Network Marketing companies have different types of Compensation Plans, as well as bonuses that may or may not be a permanent feature of each company. A Compensation Plan is similar to a salary package structure in a job environment. It tells you exactly how much you will earn, how often, and as a result of doing what. A Compensation Plan enables you to set goals for yourself, knowing exactly how your remuneration will look when you attain certain sales volumes, team building levels, or both. When investigating a Network Marketing opportunity, it is important to familiarize yourself with that company's Compensation Plan, and how it differs from other Compensation Plans in the market.

Some Compensation Plans can be quite complicated. I would advise you not to study all the Compensation Plans first in order to make your decision about what Network Marketing Company you want to join. Instead, consider the product line of the company and whether or not it makes sense in the market. It does not matter how good the Compensation Plan is, if you're not passionate about the product or service being offered to the market, or if you would not feel comfortable promoting the product or service, for whatever reason—then it would be difficult to benefit from even the "best "Compensation Plan.

Once you tick the product/service test, then you can enquire about the company's Compensation Plan. Someone should be able to explain it to you in simple terms, so that it's not difficult for you to explain it to the next person, because the Network Marketing business is a business of duplication. Secondly, it should tick certain fundamentals, which we will discuss below.

CHARACTERISTICS OF A GOOD COMPENSATION PLAN

The word good in this context can be both subjective and objective. Any good Compensation Plan should be good both subjectively (i.e. for you as an individual) and objectively (i.e. in the opinion of industry experts).

- From an objective point of view:
  - o A good Compensation Plan should have a proven track record. Track record is really anything more than 3-5 years, preferably longer. A track record gives you confidence that the company's business model is suitable for its product line or service offering, therefore the company is likely to be in a reasonably good financial position to provide you with a stable long-term business.

- o A good Network Marketing Company will be financially transparent and able to provide you with a breakdown of their Compensation Plan, as well as their Income Disclosure Statement.
- o The company should ideally not be over-leveraged (i.e. it's debt to equity ratio should be very low). Just as you would apply this test to an investment in a traditional company, you should apply this test to a Network Marketing company as well. Remember, network marketing is just a business model; the company should still be able to compete with other companies in the same industry.
- o The Compensation Plan should reward the development and maintenance of customers, as this is the only way the company makes revenue, and the only way to create passive income in time. Additionally, the Compensation Plan should reward hard work, regardless of when you come into the business. It should not matter when or where you entered the company's compensation structure, you should have the same earning opportunity as everyone else.

- From a subjective point of view, the important thing for you is to understand the Compensation Plan of the Network Marketing Company you consider joining, after you have ticked the product/service test, and consider whether or not the Compensation Plan is practical for the time you are initially able to realistically invest in the business.

Considering that the vast majority of people are unable to leave their existing jobs or traditional businesses initially, it is probably more pragmatic to look at opportunities geared for part time, with an option of going full time once the financial gain has reached a certain level that enables you to transition from full time employment/traditional business to a Network Marketing business. Even though this advice may not apply to everyone reading this book, I'm confident it will apply to the majority.

CONCLUSION

The next two chapters of the book will be dedicated to the actual Network Marketing Compensation Plan, as well as the different types available in the market. As you learn about these, consider the discussion on this chapter about the characteristics of a good Compensation Plan, in general and specifically for you. Keep in mind that all Compensation Plans, like anything in life, have a set of pros and cons. There is no perfect choice, but there are certainly going to be better choices.

5

THE NETWORK MARKETING COMPENSATION PLAN

I have to warn you that this chapter and the next are going to be the most technical in the book; however, it is necessary for me to explain the Network Marketing terminology in order for you to better understand the business model.

THE COMPENSATION PLAN

Compensation plans are basically the way in which you get paid in a Network Marketing business, therefore it is important that you understand how they work. In this chapter I will help you to understand the Network Marketing Compensation Plan and specifically discuss the 4 basic compensation structures used by Network Marketing companies. The next chapter will discuss the characteristics, as well as the pros and cons of each Compensation Plan, as well as help you to identify the best Compensation Plan FOR YOU.

The 4 basic Compensation Plans are:

- The Binary Plan

- The Breakaway Plan

- The Matrix Plan

- The Uni-Level Plan

Despite the fact that every Network Marketing Company's Compensation Plan is different, most plans are based on one of the 4 basic structures. The main difference between the Compensation Plans using the same structure is that they vary in the commissions paid, and in additional bonuses.

Due to the fact that the 4 basic Compensation Plans have differences as well as similarities, not all the information discussed in this chapter will be relevant to every plan; this is a generic explanation of a Compensation Plan. We will discuss each of the four basic plans in the next chapter.

Below is a discussion and explanation of basic Network Marketing terms that you need to understand in order to make sense of any Network Marketing Compensation Plan. The intention is that at the end of this chapter, I will have demystified these terms for you and you will be quite comfortable with having a conversation using them. Additionally, understanding these terms should make it easier for you to understand any Compensation Plan within the Network Marketing industry.

Sponsor – The sponsor is the person who introduces and signs you up with their Network Marketing Company. This is the person who should also ensure that you receive adequate training and support to help you succeed. He/she is not responsible for training you; they are responsible for showing you how to access the training.

Distributors, Representatives or Associates – Distributors, Representatives or Associates are the voluntary "sales force" of the Network Marketing Company. You join this sales force when you sign the paperwork, buy a Business Centre (explained below) and join the Network Marketing Company.

Business Centre – When you join a Network Marketing company as a Distributor, Representative or Associate, your joining fee is used to buy you a Business Centre, which gives you access to the company's Intellectual Property as well as enables you to track your organization, get your compensation, as well as anything else related to building your business. Your business or organization refers to both yourself and all the members (distributors) that you and your team have sponsored. Think of your organization as a traditional company structure with your business as the holding company and the businesses of people joining under you as subsidiaries. Typically a holding company owns a percentage of its subsidiaries, and consequently is entitled to a portion of the profits a subsidiary makes. Similarly, in a Network Marketing company, even though the structure is not an ownership structure, your business is entitled to a portion of the profits of all the businesses that have been formed by distributors you have sponsored. The diagram below illustrates both a Business Centre and your organization.

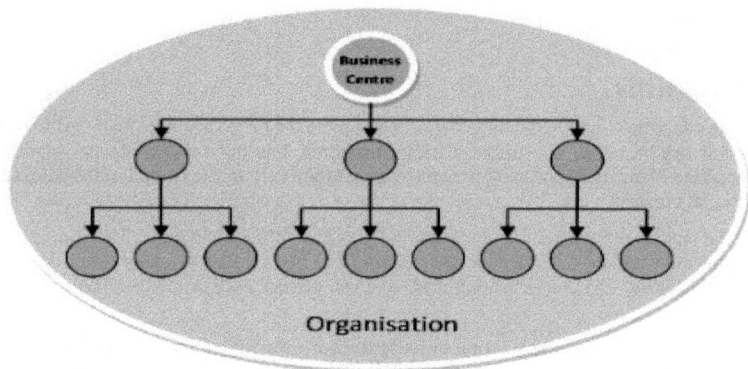

Upline – This refers to everyone sponsored directly above you. These people are responsible for providing you training and support in order to help you succeed.

Downline – This refers to individuals you have sponsored and are positioned below you in the compensation structure. Although each downline distributor is essentially owning and operating his or her business independently, it is in your interest to support them because as discussed above, you benefit from all their sales activities.

Width – This refers to the maximum number frontline members you can have. Frontline is simply the distributors that are placed immediately after you in the compensation structure.

Depth – This refers to the depth to which you can earn a commission as a result of the work done by your downline. It is obviously impractical to expect that you can get a portion of the commission made to infinite levels deep in your organization without the money running out. This is why there are caps in company ranks; nobody can practically earn commissions to infinite levels deep. I will discuss this further when I talk about the different Compensation Plans, particularly the Binary.

Level – Level refers to the position of a distributor in a downline, relative to an upline distributor. The diagram below illustrates this concept. The 9 distributors highlighted are 2nd level distributors because they sit 2 levels below the Business Centre in the compensation structure. Consequently, the non-highlighted frontline distributors are 1st level distributors.

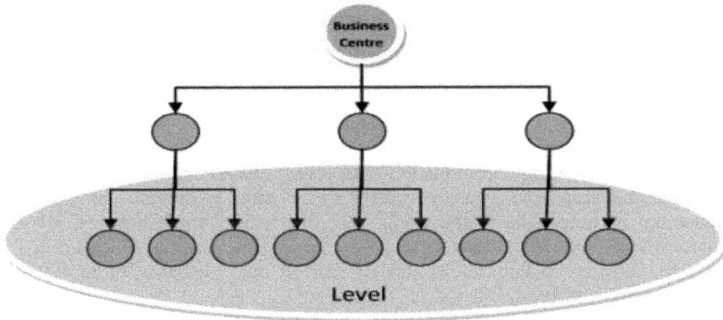

Crossline – Distributors on the same level (e.g. Frontline distributors) are referred to as crossline. Though these distributors fall under the same Business Centre, their work efforts do not benefit one another because they are in different organisations.

Legs – Every frontline or first level distributor you sponsor into your organization forms a new leg. The diagram below illustrates the concept of legs. The number of legs in your organization is determined by the number of frontline distributors you have or are allowed to have. In the illustration below, there are 3 legs formed by the 3 frontline distributors (there is a middle leg and 2 outside legs). Regardless of how many frontline distributors are allowed in a Compensation Plan, the legs are always numbered from left to right. The legs are different organizations (almost like subsidiaries of your Business Centre) being run by your frontline distributors.

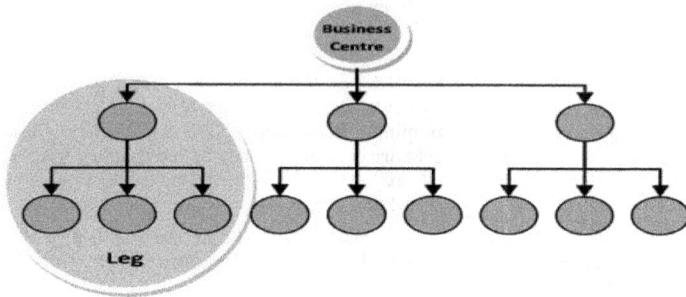

Point Value – Regardless of the kind of industry you work in, the main goal of that industry is to sell a product or service. The Network Marketing industry is no different. For every product sold in Network Marketing, a predetermined portion of the profit is paid to the team of distributors who were responsible for the sale.

Given that most Network Marketing companies operate in a number of different countries around the world, the easiest and fairest way to pay distributors commission is to use a point system. This system is used by most, but not all Network Marketing companies. Each product has an assigned point value and the volume of points that flow through your organization determines your commission. This way it doesn't matter what country you operate your business from, you are entitled to the same commission as your fellow colleagues on the other side of the world. For this reason, some Network Marketing companies who do not use the point system pay commissions in one currency, normally US Dollars; the company would not ordinarily convert the payments to local country currencies at payout stage.

Commissions – The ultimate way you earn in a Network Marketing business is through commission for sales volumes (in points or otherwise). This volume is multifold and will be covered in the section below. But basically, it covers personal as well as team sales volumes. So the greater your sales volumes, the higher your commission.

Total volume is calculated differently for each Compensation Plan structure; however, they all normally take into account *level volume* (volume by each level of your business), *leg volume* (volume by each leg in your business), *group volume* (volume by the entire organization), and *carryover volume* (volume not paid in the last pay period for whatever reason):

Variable Level Commissions - The diagram below illustrates the difference between consistent and variable commissions. Of the four basic Compensation Plans, 3 (The Breakaway, Uni-Level and the Matrix Plans) usually offer a variable commission rate for each level of distributors within your organization.

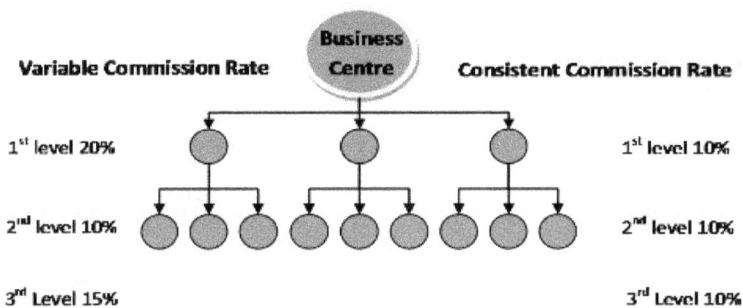

The above example illustrates that if your Compensation Plan was offering variable commission, you would receive 20% commission based on the first level volume, 10% commission based on the second level volume, and 15% commission based on the third level volume.

Alternatively, if the Compensation Plan were offering a consistent commission rate, then you would earn the same commission percentage for each level. For example, in the above diagram you would earn a 10% commission from all 3 levels. Of the 4 basic Compensation Plans, only the Binary System almost exclusively uses a consistent commission rate. This is touted as one of the advantages of the Binary System because the consistent commission rate is easier to understand

Ranks– Network Marketing companies don't only reward you with commission, they also recognize you for building a big organization resulting in larger volumes of sales going through your organization consistently. This recognition is called Ranks. Different Ranks come with different perks and the higher you advance in Ranks, the bigger the perks. These perks usually include bigger residual income and some bonuses that people in lower ranks don't qualify for.

Commonly used Rank advancements include the following in order: - Leader, Director, Bronze Director, Silver Director, Gold Director, Ruby Director, Emerald Director and the highest being the Diamond Director. Even though Rank names may differ from company to company, Rank advancements are not only recognized within your own Network Marketing, they are recognized industry wide.

Bonuses – Many Network Marketing companies offer bonuses as part of their Compensation Plan as a way of attracting people to join their business. These bonuses are normally in the form of a bigger incentives, in cash and otherwise, including car and travel bonuses. In most Network Marketing companies, these bonuses are normally reserved for top achievers, however, that is not necessarily the norm any longer. I have personally experienced some of these bonuses well before I reached any rank in my company.

CONCLUSION

Now that we are on the same page with regards to our understanding of the Network Marketing Compensation Plan, we are going to in the next chapter tackle each of the 4 basic Compensation Plans in a quest to help you understand both the subjective and the objective pros and cons of each one.

6

DIFFERENT NETWORK MARKETING COMPENSATION PLANS

Once you have done the exercise discussed in chapter 4—that of ensuring you are happy with the product or service you are going to be bringing to the market—you need to familiarize yourself with the Compensation plan of the Network Marketing company you are considering, and check whether you believe you are capable of meeting the company's requirements for a successful venture. Establishing your frontline is often considered to be the first milestone, therefore a good question to ask might be 'how many people do I personally need to sponsor to establish my frontline, and earn my first commission?'

Because the Unilevel and Breakaway plans have unlimited width restrictions, you will generally be required to personally sponsor a larger number of frontline distributors (when compared with other Compensation Plans) in order to earn a good income, therefore these plans are best suited for those who are confident they can recruit many new distributors after joining.

With the Binary Plan and some narrow Matrix Plans, there is generally less emphasis placed on personally recruiting new distributors (in other words, you don't have to personally recruit as many new distributors to fulfil your frontline), but instead there is generally more effort required in helping (training and support) new distributors establish their business. The Binary and narrow Matrix plans are generally more supportive and rewarding for building teamwork. Companies using these Compensation Plans are usually very supportive with regards to training support (so the training is not left to you, the sponsor; rather getting your team to training is the key).

We will now dedicate the rest of this chapter to discussing the 4 basic Compensation Plans, then at the end of this chapter you should be able to confidently make an informed decision about the type of Compensation Plan that you would most likely be comfortable with when choosing a Network Marketing company. But remember, product/service first, and Compensation Plan thereafter.

THE BINARY COMPENSATION PLAN

Despite the fact that the Binary Plan is relatively new to the Network Marketing industry (approximately 20 years in existence), it is quite a popular choice among both Network Marketing companies and members within the industry. The original versions of this compensation plan had some of flaws that the older compensation plans had, but companies using this plan have over time perfected it to the extent that it is very difficult to critique it.

The Binary Plan is one of the easiest Compensation Plans to explain, which is one of the reasons for its popularity among all types of participants in the industry; including new and part time participants. Below are some additional reasons for this Compensation Plan of choice for many in the industry.

The mechanics of a Binary Compensation Plan

The Binary Plan is derived from the number two (bi), which represents the maximum number of frontline associates that any Business Centre can have. Any additional distributors must then be placed under one of the two frontline members, as illustrated in the diagram below.

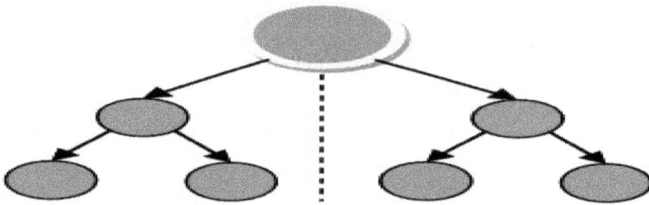

This creates a very supportive environment for new members. The easiest way for associates to achieve success is by assisting their new members in building their organisations. This team approach makes the Binary Plan incredibly attractive because there is plenty support (both initial and ongoing), since all associates within your organisation work towards achieving a common goal.

The earning potential in a binary Compensation Plan is increased by balancing the amount of leg volume flowing through either side of your Business Centre. For example, if you had $11,000 sales volume flowing through the left leg of your business, but only $9,000 sales volume flowing through the right in the same period, you are paid out on the highest common denominator for that period; which would be $9,000 in this case. What typically happens with the difference of $2,000 sales volume is that it becomes carry over volume for the next pay period; this is one of the improvements of modern day binary compensation plans. In the older versions of this compensation plan, you would lose out on the $2,000 sales volume left over from your strong leg.

Coming back to our example; so if the following period, your left sales volume is $9,500 and your right volume is $13,000, you will be paid on the lowest common denominator of $11,500 ($9,500 PLUS carried over $2,000), then there will be a carried over volume of $1,500 for the next pay period for the right leg.

Because the goal is to balance the volume flowing through your organization, this encourages associates to help their weaker downline members to build their organization, promoting teamwork and thus achieving a better volume balance, resulting in a more consistent and higher commission payout.

There are normally no depth restrictions to the binary structure and each level of your organization is paid out on a consistent commission percentage, making it easy to understand. One of the main distinctions of the Binary Plan is that it is volume-driven, as opposed to level-driven, which means it is not necessary to have a large organization to be successful. You just need to have big sales volumes. This also means there is an incentive to help new associates in your organization, no matter how deep they are.

Because there are no depth restrictions to the Binary Plan, each Business Centre has a limited earning potential, which maxes out to ensure that both distributors and the company earn a profit. So, if each Business Centre has a limit on earning potential, how is it possible that millions of dollars are being earned through Network Marketing businesses using this Binary Plan?

The answer lies in the ability to operate more than one Business Centre (usually unlimited). Once you have achieved a certain level with your Network Marketing business, where your organization has maxed out, or has limited potential to earn you more money, the company rewards the distributor with a new Business Centre. This is much like operating a supermarket and letting it grow to maturity, where growth rates have now stabilized and earning potential has reached a ceiling. The only way for you to expand and increase your earning potential is to buy or build another supermarket.

The company is happy because they have an experienced, successful distributor opening another business centre, and the distributor is happy because now they have a higher earning potential. The more business centres the distributor has, the greater the earning potential of the distributor.

Who is best suited for the Binary Compensation Plan?

Studies conducted into the Network Marketing industry have shown that the average Network Marketing distributor sponsors between 2 and 3 new distributors into their business. These findings mean that it would be hard for the 'average distributor' to be successful using some of the older compensation models where distributors were required to recruit at least 6 or more frontline distributors in order to see a return. However, regardless of the fact that requirement for success is quite low in a binary Compensation Plan, a serious Network Marketing business builder, is likely to focus on a much higher number of personal recruits in order to increase the probability of extreme success in his/her business.

The Binary Plan was created to give a level playing field for all to increase the probability of success, not only the superstars. Because the Binary Compensation Structure only allows
31

the sponsoring of 2 frontline distributors, and *normally* requires only the frontline level in order to start earning, even your less-than-average network marketer still has the potential to achieve financial freedom using this model. Therefore, the Binary Plan is suitable to even the average network marketer.

THE MATRIX COMPENSATION PLAN

The Matrix Plan has a set width and depth for which distributors are compensated.

There are many variations to this Compensation Plan but the basic structure is normally identified by a simple equation that includes the width and the depth of the plan. The diagram below illustrates a plan that has a width of 3 and a depth of at least 2. So if the diagram below was illustrating a 3 x 6 plan, it would mean that you can only sponsor a maximum of 3 frontline distributors illustrated, and you have the potential to earn commissions up to 4 more levels deep, because the total levels deep you can earn in a 3x6 is 6.

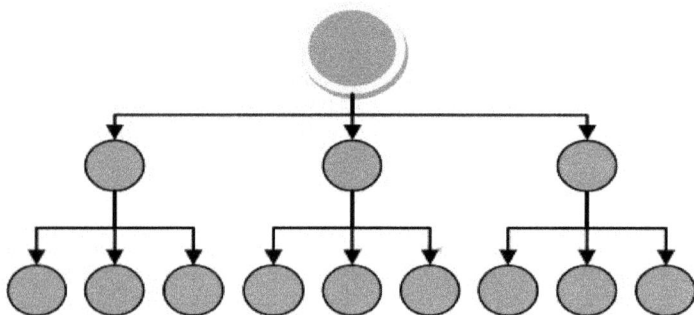

So if you personally recruit more people after your frontline is full, there is no choice but to place these new distributors under your frontline as their frontline distributors, a process referred to as "spillover", which is also used in the Binary Plan. In most modern Matrix Plans, the sponsor can decide where in their downline they place the "spillover," which gives them control over how they strategically build their organization and team.

One of the main advantages of the Matrix Plan over the Unilevel Plan and the Breakaway Plan (discussed below), is once your frontline is full, your focus now changes towards developing your frontline distributors; assisting them to find and train their frontline distributors, and so on, that is where the teamwork element and support comes in.

A potential setback of the Matrix Plan is that generally the amount of commissions paid on each level is variable. Therefore, there is more incentive for distributors to assist some levels of their downline, but not others. Additionally, some plans are quite wide and may require you to fill six or more frontline positions before assisting your frontline in developing their own organization. As a consequence, another drawback to the variable commission rate is that while it does offer some incentives, it can be hard to explain to potential prospects.

When reviewing Compensation Plans, in particular the different Matrix structures, you should be aware that the narrower and deeper the plan, the more supportive your upline distributors will be. For example a 2 x 12 plan (which is more like a binary, just with limited depth) encourages more teamwork and support from upline distributors than a 6 x 5 plan.

To make this Compensation Plan more attractive, some companies have added extra compensation, e.g. "infinity bonuses" which allow above average distributors to earn commissions on levels specified outside the depth of the plan. Because every Compensation Plan is different, we won't go into these details, as they are not necessarily applicable to all Matrix Plans. It is safe to say that they are just additional rewards. It should, however, be considered that whilst a number of these bonuses are very attractive, only a small percentage of distributors are typically successful enough to earn them. However, because the type of person reading this book is someone looking for TIME & FINANCIAL FREEDOM, it is unlikely that you will be an average distributor.

In summary, the Matrix Compensation Plans have the potential to be very rewarding to both newcomers and Network Marketing Entrepreneurs, particularly once you get to understand the compensation structure in its entirety. For an example, if the Matrix Plan is not a Forced Matrix Plan (i.e. does not restrict the number of legs), there is higher likelihood of long-term success even though there are still restrictions on the levels for which one is compensated. Like most compensation structures, this model does offer the potential to earn a high income if structured correctly.

THE BREAKAWAY COMPENSATION PLAN

This Compensation Plan was one of the original Network Marketing Compensation Plans and is still used by a number of Pioneer Network Marketing companies today. Given that this structure has been around for many years and has a proven track record, start-up companies still commonly implement it as well. However, just like all compensation structures, whilst there are some advantages to this compensation structure, there are also a number of disadvantages, which will be discussed in this section.

The name Breakaway is derived from the concept that distributors climb the ladder of success and when they reach a certain level, as illustrated in the diagram below; they are allowed to break away from their upline distributors and run their organization independently. As distributors break away from their upline, they are allowed them to earn a greater commission.

This compensation plan shares a number of similarities with the Unilevel Plan (to be discussed later in the chapter) in that each distributor is only allowed to sponsor one level of distributors (frontline). Whilst there is no limit to the width (number of frontline distributors) in which you can sponsor, the Breakaway Plan offers limited incentive for teamwork within your organization, and the competition between cross line distributors can make it difficult to recruit people close to you into this structure because they are "rivals" or competitors.

As with all Network Marketing companies, the main goal for each business associate is to distribute the parent company's products. This is best achieved in the Breakaway Plan by recruiting as many frontline distributors as you can who personally consume and /or sell your company's product, and then encourage them to do the same.

The Breakaway

Breaking away from your upline has numerous benefits to the individual distributor, such as earning a higher commission rate; however it can have a serious negative impact to the organization from which you break away. By breaking away, the volume that your upline previously received from you no longer flows through your upline's business at the same rate.

As distributor's breakaway, the original sponsor is still entitled to earn a small percentage from each break away distributors' efforts. This is referred to as an *override commission*. Each breakaway organization is referred to as a *generation* and although distributors are

34

entitled to earn an override commission on all of their breakaway generations, unfortunately this override commission is only a small fraction in comparison to the commissions they were earning previously.

Another setback with the Breakaway Plan is that although you may have reached the level where you are allowed to break away from your upline and earn greater commission, your organization will grow and distributors in your downline may also qualify to break away from you. Although initially having a distributor break away from your organization can put a dent in your short-term income, creating a number of breakaway organizations can help you earn a long-term residual income and re-focus your time towards developing a frontline of future leaders.

In general, this plan is most suited to those distributors who are confident in their ability to recruit new distributors and have good management skills. For those looking at this Compensation Plan for the first time, one thing to consider is that you may experience a lack of support from your upline distributors once you are established and that you will be working in competition with other crossline distributors. Whilst the potential commissions can be very rewarding with this compensation structure, the Binary Plan and the Matrix Plan are generally considered friendlier and more supportive for newcomers.

In years gone by, some companies who used the Breakaway Plans gave the industry a bad name. These particular companies set the group sales volume with unrealistic targets, where new distributors were encouraged to purchase extra product to assist their upline to earn a commission. Consequently, many distributors ended up being stuck with stock they could not sell. High hopes were drummed into some of the distributors that led them into financial trouble. I have personally experienced this and it resulted in me walking away from the industry for years. Fortunately, this apparently rarely happens today.

Another setback to the Breakaway Plan is that it is hard for many to understand and even harder to try and explain it to your prospects.

Despite the above discussion, the Breakaway Plan does have a number of advantages. It has a good track record, which makes it attractive to new companies looking for a proven business model. In particular, the Breakaway Plan works in favour of those distributors who have good selling or recruiting skills. Some might argue that this Compensation Plan is more suited to the full timers, however recent advancements in the industry, particularly the internet, can make it just as friendly to the part-time distributors.

THE UNILEVEL COMPENSATION PLAN

The Unilevel plan has been around for many years and given its proven track record is still used by a number of Network Marketing companies today. The main benefit to this model is that it is very easy to understand, however, like all Compensation Plans, whilst there are some benefits; there are also a number of disadvantages that should also be considered.

Unilevel, as the name suggests, only enables you to sponsor one line of distributors (as illustrated below), therefore everyone you sponsor is on your frontline.

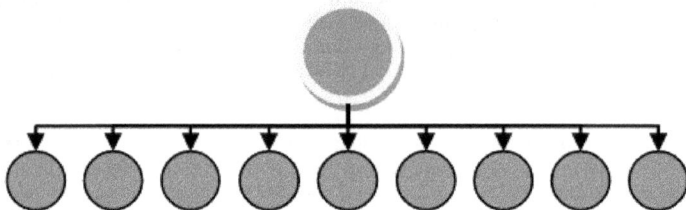

There are no width limitations to this plan (i.e. there is no limit to the number of people you can sponsor in your frontline) and commissions are normally paid out on a limited depth—common plans that we have reviewed pay commissions between 5 and 7 levels deep. Therefore, the common goal of this plan is to recruit a large number of frontline distributors and then encourage them to do the same.

To earn a commission using this structure, there is normally only a minimal amount of personal volume required, which essentially makes it easier for part-timers to earn an income. Although it tends to be easier to earn a commission using this compensation structure, when comparing it to other plans, the structure itself restricts the total amount of each commission you can earn (i.e. although it is easier to earn commissions you do not tend to earn as much).

One of the main disadvantages of the plan is that every distributor you sponsor becomes crossline to all of your other frontline distributors, and therefore must work in competition with the others. This can present numerous challenges for the newcomer who attempts to recruit friends and family into their business. In essence, they will be working in competition with one another. An ever-increasing frontline also requires continual training and the management of large numbers of people.

The Unilevel plan does, however, have a few advantages, mainly the fact that it is easy to explain. Generally, the more distributors you recruit, the greater your commission payout. This makes it attractive to your experienced network marketers, particularly those who are serious about their business and have the ability to develop management and training systems for their growing downline.

Given the competition created between frontline distributors within this compensation structure, it is common practice for distributors within this plan to target their cold market (people they don't know) as a way to build their organization. This may include developing lead generation systems and the use of Internet leads.

Most modern Network Marketing companies using this model have made slight changes to its basic structure to make it more attractive and allow some partial teamwork. Additionally, most Unilevel plans now also include a number of bonuses to make their Compensation Plan more appealing. Another advantage of modern day Unilevel plans is that when distributors rank advance, they are generally entitled to earn a higher commission rate.

This compensation model is generally best suited for those who have Network Marketing experience or those who are very confident in their ability to recruit a large number of frontline distributors. Like most compensation structures, this model does offer the potential to earn a very high income if you are willing to put in the work.

CONCLUSION

I'm sure you would agree that there are pros and cons to each Compensation Plan, with more pros than cons for others and vice a versa. However, as discussed in chapter 4, in order to make your decision about which Network Marketing Company you want to join, first consider the product line of the company. It does not matter how good the Compensation Plan is, if you're not passionate about the products or services you have to offer, and/or you would not feel comfortable promoting them, it would be difficult to reap the rewards of even the best Compensation Plan.

It is also vital to understand the Compensation Plan of the Network Marketing Company you consider joining and consider whether or not it is practical for the time you are initially able to realistically spend on the business.

So in conclusion, I would encourage you to pick a Network Marketing Company that not only provides you with the best opportunity, but one that is also supportive of your team members. I cannot emphasize enough though that the product being offered by the company should be something you are passionate enough about to share with others continuously; something you are not likely to get tired of talking about, and something that is so well positioned in the market that it is likely to be relevant for a very long time to come.

7

WHO SUPPORTS NETWORK MARKETING

This chapter is dedicated to demonstrating the credibility of the Network Marketing business model by sharing with you some of the things being said by well-known and well-respected business people in society, whom you have probably not only heard of, but follow closely, and whose books and other material you probably have in your library at home. Human nature is sometimes such that a truth spoken by an unknown figure does not have the same impact as the same truth spoken by a well-respected figure in society.

I would be erring if all I did in this book was reveal to you the truth about Network Marketing, no matter how truthful that truth is, without backing it with the same truth being told by well-respected figures in our society—who have carefully studied the industry, compared it with other business models, and come to the conclusion that it is actually one of the best, if not the best business model, available to ordinary people today. Because we work with human beings who have the characteristics I mentioned in the first paragraph above, this chapter of the book is important for both you and me as we go about running our Network Marketing businesses.

Below are some of the well-known and well-respected names in our society who are either explicit supporters of Network Marketing, or believe in principles that are found in the Network Marketing business model. The names include, but are not limited to Donald Trump, Robert Kiyosaki, Zig Ziglar, Jim Rohn and Tony Robbins.

These are not the only people who are supporters of Network Marketing, but for the sake of integrity of information, we will only use quotes from books and official websites of some of the above-mentioned people. The rest of this chapter will be dedicated to showing you some of the things they say about Network Marketing.

In their co-authored book entitled, *Why we want You to be Rich*, Donald Trump and Robert Kiyosaki have dedicated a whole chapter to the topic of Why they Support Network Marketing. Below are some of the things they say in that chapter.

Donald Trump – Entrepreneur and Best Selling Author

"I did not know much about Network Marketing and the direct sales industry, but when a friend told me it was one of the fastest growing business models, I had to open my mind and look into it. What I found surprised me."

"Years ago, many people were opposed to a business model known as franchising. Many people questioned the legitimacy of franchising. Today, everyone in the world knows about McDonalds. Network Marketing, being a new business model, is experiencing the same opposition franchising experienced years ago."

"Looking into this industry, I was surprised to find many major Fortune 500 companies have added a Network Marketing component to their business. Today many banks, telecom companies, real estate brokerages, credit card companies, and major consumer brands are committed to this new form of people to people marketing and distribution. So my recommendation is to keep an open mind, and if you are looking to start your own business, a Network Marketing business might be for you."

"Network marketing has proven itself to be a viable and rewarding source of income, and the challenges could be just right for you. There have been some remarkable examples of success, and those successes have been earned through diligence, enthusiasm, and the right product combined with timing."

Robert Kiyosaki – Entrepreneur and Best Selling Author

"Long term success in life requires a reflection of your education, life experience and personal character. Many Network Marketing companies provide personal development training in those key areas."

"I recommend a Network Marketing business. I recommend the industry for people who want to change and get the necessary skills and attitude training to be successful in the B (Business) Quadrant."

"Where could you find a business that will invest the time in your education, your personal development and building your own business? The answer is: most Network Marketing businesses."

"Building a B Quadrant business[2] is not an easy task. So you need to ask yourself, 'Do I have what it takes? Am I willing to go beyond my comfort zone? Am I willing to be led and willing to learn to lead? Is there a very rich person inside of me, ready to come out?' If the answer is Yes, start looking for a Network Marketing business that has a great training program."

"A Network Marketing business is a B Quadrant business because it meets several criteria I look for in a business or investment. Those criteria are; leverage, control, creativity, expandability and predictability. Additional positive characteristics of a Network Marketing

---

2

[2] "Forbes defines a big business owner, a B quadrant business owner, as a person who controls a business with more than 500 employees."

business are; tax breaks increase, you meet like-minded people, it allows you to take time, Network Marketing businesses are patient, and you get to leverage the systems that are already in place."

"I'm often asked if Network Marketing is a Pyramid Scheme. My reply is that corporations really are pyramid schemes. A corporation has only one person at the top, generally the CEO, and everyone else below.

A true Network Marketing business is the exact opposite of a traditional business model. The Network Marketing business is designed to bring you to the top, not keep you at the bottom. A true Network Marketing business does not succeed unless it brings people to the top."

Below are some of the additional things that Robert Kiyosaki says in his book entitled, ***The Business of the 21st Century***.

"If I had to do it all over again and start from scratch, rather than build an old-style business, I would start out by building a Network Marketing business."

"Today, many Network Marketing companies are spreading peace through economic opportunity all over the world. Not only are Network Marketing companies thriving in all the major capitals of the world, but many are also working in developing nations, bringing financial hope to millions of people who live in impoverished countries. Most traditional corporations can only survive where people are rich and have money to spend. It is time that people all over the world had an equal opportunity to enjoy a rich and abundant life, rather than spend their lives working hard only to make the rich richer. It's time YOU had that opportunity. Welcome to the 21st century."

"Network marketing offers a path to personal success, to building great wealth and creating financial freedom through a process that operates successfully only through helping out fellow human beings. You can become rich by being cheap and greedy. You can also become rich by being abundant and generous. "

"By its very nature and design, Network Marketing is a strikingly fair, democratic, socially responsible system of generating wealth."

"Network Marketing is a revolutionary form of business: For the first time in history, it is now possible for anyone and everyone to share in the wealth that, until now, has been reserved only for the chosen few or the lucky."

"In the years ahead, I expect to see an explosion in the prevalence, penetration, visibility, and maturation of leading Network Marketing companies."

"For a world with less and less of its former security, Network Marketing is emerging as a new engine of individual achievement and security. Network Marketing gives millions of people throughout the world the opportunity to take control of their lives and financial futures."

"Network Marketing is more than just a good idea; in many ways, it is the business model of the future. Why? Because the world is finally starting to awaken to the reality that the Industrial Age is over."

"Most Network Marketing companies care primarily about how much you are willing to learn, to change and grow, and whether you have the guts to stick it out through thick and thin, while you learn to be a business owner."

"A Network Marketing system is set up to make it possible for anyone to share in the acquisition of wealth. This is a very democratic way of wealth creation. The system is open to anyone who has drive, determination, and perseverance. The system does not really care what college you went to or whether you want to one at all. It does not care how much money you are making today, what race or sex you are, how good looking you are, who your parents are, or how popular you are."

"One reason I have such strong respect for Network Marketing is that it is a genuine equal opportunity business."

"The number one reason I recommend Network Marketing is for its system of real world business education and personal development."

"Network Marketing gives you the opportunity to face your fears, deal with them, overcome them, and bring out the winner that you have living inside you."

"Today, Network Marketing is recognized by many experts and accomplished business people as one of the fastest-growing business models in the world."

CONCLUSION

There you have it ladies and gentlemen, from the mouths of Millionaires and Billionaires. I have for the sake of brevity not quoted all the things that have been said by the figures mentioned at the beginning of this chapter. Some of the quotes by the likes of Tony Robbins and Zig Ziglar have been used to support some of the discussion points throughout the book.

Some of the above mentioned entrepreneurs and other well known ones own, or have owned/ invested in Network Marketing companies themselves, e.g. Donald Trump's Trump Network, and Warren Buffett's Pampered Chef.

It is clear from the above quotes and discussions that Networking Marketing is a credible business model of the future as understood and strongly supported by well-known successful people in our society. I trust this chapter has assisted you in your decision to participate in this incredible opportunity of Network Marketing.

As a way of keeping the discussions on this topic alive, we have decided to hold regular book reading sessions initially in Johannesburg, South Africa. These book-reading sessions entitled *The Reading Room* will be held as often as weekly for approximately 90 minutes and will only be accessible for FREE to those who have purchased this book. It will be a requirement for people to have read the relevant chapter of discussion before *The Reading Room* session in order to derive maximum value from the discussions. One chapter will be discussed during each session, as well as the life and wealth creation principles discussed in that particular chapter. Participants will be allowed to bring in additional literature to support or challenge the principles discussed in that chapter because the intention of these sessions is to bring like-minded people together in order for them to learn from each other and grow in their endeavours of pursuing TIME & FINANCIAL FREEDOM.

The discussions will be held with the author and from time to time with well-respected guest speakers in the areas of wealth creation and life balance. The intention is for one group to stay together from chapter 1 through to chapter 10 over a 10-week period, followed by another group, and so on and so forth. Participation will include light homework and accountability to the group; therefore participants need to know they will be able to commit to all 10 sessions and do the homework involved. Should one fall off the group for arbitrary reasons, the group may decide that they will not be allowed to re-enter the next group. Participation is on a first come first serve basis, so quickly go and register on www.TheTruthAboutNetworkMarketingRevealed.com/bonuses.

The Reading Room sessions will also be available to those residing outside of Johannesburg and South Africa via webinar; you just have to choose the webinar option when you go to www.TheTruthAboutNetworkMarketingRevealed.com/bonuses.

8

WHY PEOPLE FAIL IN NETWORK MARKETING

There are several reasons why people fail in Network Marketing and we will be discussing a few prominent ones in this chapter. Some of the reasons include lack of passion for the product, lack of seriousness about the business and unrealistic expectations.

- **Lack of passion for the product**

One of the main reasons people fail in Network Marketing, as discussed in Chapters 4, 5, and 6, is the fact that they don't become a product of the product. What I'm referring to here is passion about the product or service they are offering the market. Our discussions in Chapters 4, 5 and 6 were centred around the importance of the Network Marketing Compensation Plan, but we made it very clear in that discussion, time and time again, that it does not matter how good the Compensation Plan is, if you are not passionate about the product you are offering the market, and if you yourself are not the user of the product, you cannot be convincing to the next person about its positive attributes.

- **Lack of seriousness about the business**

Another reason people fail in Network Marketing is the double-edged sword of the low barriers to entry of this industry; this is both a curse and a blessing as discussed in the introductory chapter. It is a blessing because you are able to start most Network Marketing businesses with less than $1,000 investment (including product), often much less than that, however, it's a curse because due to that very fact, many people joining this industry treat it as a hobby, rather than a legitimate business. They don't invest time and money in their personal development and when their small initial compensation dries up; they complain that it's not working. They easily give up because the investment made was not much anyway.

Their statistics then have to go into annual reports of their Network Marketing companies and skew the results of the ability of masses to make money from the business, because they either earned nothing since they registered as a Business Associate/Representative, or they earned very little. This gives a bad name to Network Marketing companies because often, Income Disclosure Statements show that on average, less than 25% (much less in other companies) of Representatives/Business Associates are making any money from the Business. The issue though is that, if people do not follow the SYSTEM (**S**aving **Y**ourself **S**ignificant **T**ime, **E**nergy and **M**oney) that the companies readily make available to EVERY Business Associate or Representative at sign up, there is nothing the companies can do because each Business Associate or Representative is running his or her own business.

If the same people had made 10 times (or more) the investment they made in their Network Marketing business in a traditional business, their attitude would be much different, even if they had 10 times the challenges they perceive of their Network Marketing business; hence the low barriers to entry is both a blessing and a curse.

- **Unrealistic expectations**

Some Representatives/Business Associates give up on their Network Marketing businesses before they even start because of unrealistic expectations about support from their Sponsor or from the organization. Some Representatives get into Network Marketing expecting a quick rich scheme, and when they realize there's work involved, they give up working on their business. The main unrealistic expectations in my opinion are perceived or real lack of support, as well as perceived or real lack of training.

   o   Lack of support

One of the most popular excuses for non-performing Representatives is that there is no support from their Sponsor. I will talk about my own experience with regards to this challenge; this may not apply to all Networking Companies because of the different Compensation Plans. However, even with different types of compensation plans, most modern day Network Marketing companies make an effort to incentivize team building

In my company, if the Sponsor is not able to give you the support you need to grow your business, for whatever reason, those above him/her in the company are more than willing to assist you in pursuing your goals with the company. What it boils down to though is that it is YOUR responsibility to find a solution to this challenge if you experience it. Even though company cultures may differ, each company will have a remedy for the problem if you proactively seek it.

   o   Lack of training

Many Network Marketing Company Representatives fail because they simply refuse to make use of the support their companies offer through training. Many companies, as soon as they establish themselves in a country or city, make it their priority to support their Representatives in those areas through regular training. These training sessions are often available to new and existing Representatives as frequently as weekly. None of us are born experts in any field until we are thoroughly trained it that field and have practiced what we have been taught hundreds and thousands of times, according to Malcolm Gladwell in his book the *Outlier, 10,000 hours*. One of the most fulfilling things about Network Marketing is that we don't have to reach the 10,000 hours of practice before we earn, we Earn While We Learn.

Many Representatives in the Network Marketing industry expect to get into this new industry and know everything, and of course they fail. The International Director of

Training in our company often says, "We are born to lose until we are taught to win." None of us are born knowing how to make money, or how to handle ourselves in our journey to making money, as well as when we have arrived at the destination of wealth acquisition. All of us need to be taught, coached and trained in this journey. As Tony Robbins says, "If you want to be successful, find someone who has achieved the results you want and copy what they do and you'll achieve the same results.

CONCLUSION

There are obviously a lot more reasons why people fail in Network Marketing than the ones discussed in the chapter, but the common thread among all of them is lack of taking responsibility by the Business Associate/Representative for his success or failure. The Network Marketing industry makes you a better person because even if you come into the industry with that attitude, you soon realize that the industry, or your company, does not owe you anything. All it is doing is giving you an opportunity; along with support to make you successful, what you do with it is your own determination. The Network Marketing Industry is an equal opportunity vehicle; it's a vehicle that levels the playing field for all. Nobody is there to work FOR you, but EVERYBODY is there to work WITH you.

Just over 10 years ago I was involved in a Network Marketing company that left me with a bad taste in my mouth and as a result I stayed away from the industry for years, until my current company. What I realized though is that there was nothing necessarily wrong with that company or its product. The company was just wrong for me. I was not passionate about the product and although millions of people were becoming Millionaires through that company, and are continuing to do so today, I was never going to join them because of all the above-mentioned reasons.

Additionally, the company's compensation plan was not structured for the person I was at the time, someone looking for part time income while I was building my career. I have learned my lesson and have grown as a person and I thank God that I came across a company that draws out the passion in me to go out every day and grow my business.

Even though I am a different person today than I was then, the old company still does not appeal to me because of the structure of its compensation plan, the relevance and pricing of its products in the market, etc.

The company associated with my current network marketing business appeals to me because I think it's revolutionizing the sector in which it operates and I can see the value it brings to the consumer when compared with its competitors. The company's products would be relevant and competitive even if it were not using the network marketing business model to promote them, which is for me the litmus test each network marketing company should pass.

9

WHY NETWORK MARKETING IS A POWERFUL TOOL TO TAKE YOU TO YOUR GOAL OF WEALTH CREATION IN A RELATIVELY SHORT SPACE OF TIME

Network Marketing is more than capable of making ANYBODY from ANY BACKGROUND wealthy in a relatively short space of time—three to five years or much less. If you were looking for a get rich quick scheme, I'm sorry to burst your bubble. Network Marketing takes some time, as many good things do, but it takes much less time than most traditional business models, and it takes much less work when compared with other business models. It's a business that cannot be done without passion. So when you find a company that you fall in love with and whose product, service, corporate culture, people and corporate image you love as well, then Network Marketing is the EASIEST business model available out there. Even though you may need to put in quite a bit of time upfront, YOU decide WHEN that time is, knowing that the more you succeed in the business, the less time you will have to spend on your business, which brings me to the topic of LEVERAGE.

NETWORK MARKETING USES LEVERAGE

As John D, Rockefeller said, "I would rather earn 1% of a 100 people's efforts, than 100% of my own efforts." Network Marketing is a business of leverage. Depending on the compensation plan involved, you are not only leveraging off the efforts of those who join after you, you are also able to leverage off the efforts of those who joined before you. The meaning of the word leverage in its simplest form is "positional advantage," or "power to act effectively," ability to get 10, 100, 1000 x results for the same effort on your part. This power of leverage makes Network Marketing one of THE most lucrative business models available in the market today.

NETWORK MARKETING REQUIRES YOU TO FOLLOW A PROVEN SYSTEM

Tony Robbins says, "If you want to be successful, find someone who has achieved the results you want and copy what they do and you'll achieve the same results." There is NO OTHER WAY to succeed in Network Marketing; it is only by COPYING, which again makes it possible for ANYONE, with whatever level of intelligence and from whatever background, to win in Network Marketing.

You do not even have to go further than your company. The top Income Earners in each Network Marketing Company make it a point to share their formula of success with as many people in their company as possible. These Top Income earners are often the trainers of the company, it is highly unlikely that someone who is not a Top Income Earner is allowed to be a trainer in a Network Marketing company. The industry believes in teaching by action and results; so if you have not walked that particular road to success, how would you know what the pitfalls and the short cuts are on that path?

So the formula is simple, follow the SYSTEM (**S**aving **Y**ourself **S**ignificant **T**ime, **E**nergy and **M**oney) that the company makes available, attend the trainings, listen to past trainings, follow your leaders, and you are bound to enjoy the same success they achieved; likely in less time than they did because you have them as pioneers.

NETWORK MARKETING IS IN THE BUSINESS OF MAKING OTHER PEOPLE'S DREAMS COME TRUE

I'm yet to come across someone who is not blessed and satisfied whenever they have an opportunity to help other people. It is such a prestigious achievement to be able to help other people in any way, and that is what the Network Marketing industry does on a daily basis. In fact, it is impossible to be selfish in Network Marketing because if you are not helping other people and sharing the business, you are simply unable to succeed. As Zig Ziglar says, "If you help enough people get what they want, you will get what you want," that's Network Marketing.

CONCLUSION

Networking Marketing companies have Compensation Plans that show you the maximum that can be made in different ranks, as well as Income Disclosure Statements that show how much money on average has been made annually by Representatives or Business Associates in different ranks. This makes it possible for you to plan your success and create goals and targets that are realistic for you. Simply put, you know exactly what you get out for what you put into your Network Marketing business.

10

7 STEPS TO ACHIEVING TIME & FINANCIAL FREEDOM ETHICALLY AND WITH CREDIBILITY

As you know, this book promised to show you how to achieve TIME and FINANCIAL FREEDOM ethically and honestly in 7 easy steps. I'm a woman of integrity, I would not forget my promise, and I would not go back on my word, so here goes.

Now that you understand what the Network Marketing industry and business model is about, and know it is a credible and honest business model supported by well known and unknown millionaires and billionaires globally, and that more often than not, one or more Network Marketing companies are in their portfolio of investments; it's time for you to make a decision about changing your life for the better, PERMANENTLY! NO MORE EXCUSES!

Einstein said that insanity is taking the same action over and over and expecting different results, I'm certain, dear reader, that you are NOT insane, so it's time to make those changes in your life and it is easily doable in 7 easy steps.

STEP 1 – DECIDE THAT NETWORK MARKETING IS THE VEHICLE THAT'S GOING TO GET YOU TO YOUR GOAL

Every success story starts with a DECISION. If you read biographies of many successful people, they will be able to tell you, to the tee, what the defining moment was in their lives, what happened, when it was, and where it was. During those trying times, they DECIDED that they are going to turn their lives around.

Now a decision on its own is not enough. According to one of my leaders, Matt Morris, the author of the best seller, Unemployed Millionaire, you need a vehicle, effort, and skill. Decide that Network Marketing is the VEHICLE that is going to take you to your TIME and FINANCIAL FREEDOM goal and JUST DO IT!

STEP 2 – CHOOSE A NETWORK MARKETING COMPANY WHOSE PRODUCT/OFFERING/CORPORATE CULTURE YOU IDENTIFY WITH IN YOUR MARKET AND MAKE SURE THAT THE COMPANY HAS A VERY STRONG SUPPORT NETWORK WITHIN YOUR MARKET

There are many ways of finding out about available Network Marketing Companies and their credentials, and whether or not they are in your market. You can interact with me on my website www.TheTruthAboutNetworkMarketingRevealed.com should you want to have further discussions or assistance about this.

This is a critical decision because it has a serious bearing on your ability to stay the course even when things are not quite where you would like them to be. You need to LOVE your company, you need to LOVE your product offering, in that way you will automatically be passionate about it, and working with it will not be work, but some serious FUN ☺.

STEP 3 – JOIN THE COMPANY YOU HAVE DECIDED ON

Once you have done step 2 and have chosen the company, joining the company should be a decision that you DO NOT DELAY, because the nature of the industry is such that the faster you get in, the more leverage you have for the rest of your life, so DO NOT PROCRASTINATE. Whatever company you choose to work with will be able to explain this to you in depth, and the consequences related to procrastination in this industry.

Besides, the barriers to entry are so crazy low that you HAVE NO EXCUSE to not join immediately, NONE!

STEP 4 – SIT DOWN WITH YOUR SPONSOR AND WORK ON GOAL SETTING WITHIN 24 TO 48 HOURS

Psychologically, you want to know your game plan and get to work (or play ☺) in 24 to 48 hours. What this does is expose you to the taste of success very early on because you are able to see your remuneration immediately once you start working. This is good for your confidence in the business and propels you to success, because let's face it, the more you see results, the more you know that you have the deal.

STEP 5 – DO EXACTLY AS YOUR SPONSOR AND YOUR LEADERS SAY, NO MATTER HOW UNCOMFORTABLE AND UNNATURAL IT IS

Now this is the most difficult part and probably the biggest challenge you are going to face in your Network Marketing career; DOING AS YOU ARE TOLD. Some of the success nuggets you are going to get from your leaders are going to feel uncomfortable, unnatural to some extent, but who has ever succeeded doing what they have been doing all along? You need to understand that this is an industry or company you are unfamiliar with and that your leaders have been there, done that, and have evidence to show their success. So not doing as they tell you will just delay your success, and you do not want that. Rather surrender from the word go and resolve that you are going to copy everything they do, because it works.

My other mentor, another bestselling Author, Loral Langemeier, the Millionaire Maker, and many other millionaires and billionaires out there, all say the same thing—find someone who has already achieved what you want to achieve, and just copy what they do, ESPECIALLY if they are willing to share their formula with you. JUST COPY THEM! The beauty about the Network Marketing industry is that copying is the VERY ESSENCE of the business model, if you don't copy; you are not going to succeed. The formula is done for you; all you need to do is to just copy it.

STEP 6 – PLUG IN TO ALL THEIR TRAINING, ATTEND EVERY POSSIBLE TRAINING EVENT

Training is CRITICAL when you join the Network Marketing industry as discussed earlier. Remember, this is something new to you, you DON'T know what you are doing, but it's easy with training. Most of these companies incentivize you in different ways to attend training because therein lies your success. Several Network Marketing companies are Personal Development companies disguised as marketing companies; the amount of personal development you get at prices that are not even a fraction of what you pay in the market is out of this world. Trust me, in my entire corporate life I have never been exposed to such amazing personal development in such a short space of time; this is the kind of training that will make you a better person, PERIOD!

STEP 7 – WATCH THE MONEY COMING IN ☺

This is my favourite part; it's so easy to make money in this industry. The compensation plans of some of these companies are some of the best. The level of meritocracy is amazing; these companies are some of the best companies in the world with regards to compensation. The greatest stimulus is that as part of your path to wealth creation, there are little and big rewards that make the path so much more enjoyable, and make it ludicrous to even consider giving up! What you put in is not what you get out, what you get out is WAY MORE than what you put in, that's the power of LEVERAGE my friend.

In many cases, people get their Return on Investment ("ROI") in a few days or a few weeks. I got 150% ROI on my investment in 4 weeks, and I was slow...

I have to advise you though; the intention is not for you to start living from the money you make from your Network Marketing Business immediately when you replace your current income. Look at this business for the long term. As Robert Kiyosaki advises in his book entitled, *The Business of the 21st Century*, you must use the money you make from your business to invest in assets that give you long-term passive income. I would personally advise you to quit your job or your current source of income ONLY when you reach that amount of money from your residual compensation of your Network Marketing Business. Remember, the medium to long term goal is TIME & FINANCIAL FREEDOM, so you want your passive income to gradually overtake your active income, that's when you can truly say you have both TIME & FINANCIAL FREEDOM, when you earn more than enough; even if you are inactive in your business for long periods of time.

CONCLUSION

Now that you have the blueprint on how to make a resounding success of your life in 3-5 years (less if you so desire), go to www.TheTruthAboutNetworkMarketingRevealed.com and claim your 4 bonuses if you have not already done so. These will enhance your understanding of the industry and/or will support you in your journey of TIME & FINANCIAL FREEDOM and make it easier for you to make your decision. I hope to see and talk to you soon.

RECOMMENDED READING

The following books have, and are continuing to help, me tremendously in my journey to TIME & FINANCIAL FREEDOM. Some I have had in my library for years and every time I read them I get new revelations. But they have never made more sense in my life than they are making now, because I am putting them to practice and boy am I reaping the rewards.

- The Millionaire Maker – by Loral Langemeier
- Yes! Energy – by Loral Langemeier
- Rich Dad Poor Dad – by Robert Kiyosaki
- The Business of the 21st Century – by Robert Kiyosaki
- Why we want You to be Rich – by Donald Trump & Robert Kiyosaki
- The Unemployed Millionaire – by Matt Morris
- Go Pro – by Eric Worre
- Double Your Income Doing What You Love – by Raymond Aaron
- Why "A" Students Work for "C" Students and Why "B" Students Work for the Government – by Robert Kiyosaki
- Think and Grow Rich – by Napoleon Hill
- The Outlier – Malcolm Gladwell

You can find links to all these books on our book website: www.TheTruthAboutNetworkMarketingRevealed.com/usefullinks&quotes. I wish for you with all my heart the success I'm experiencing, which is becoming greater and greater every single day. I'm experiencing the saying in my company that says; if you are coachable, trainable and teachable, you will be UNSTOPPABLE. I wish for you the same.

Because success starts in the mind, many of us often need some assistance with changing our mindset and self-limiting beliefs and setting ourselves up for success. No matter how powerful a vehicle the Network Marketing business model is, with self-limiting beliefs, it will be difficult to achieve the required success. If you would like some coaching, mentoring and motivation, please contact us via our website on www.TheTruthAboutNetworkMarketingRevealed.com/bonuses for a free 1st coaching session.

Happy TIME & FINANCIAL FREEDOM SEEKING!!!!!

www.ingramcontent.com/pod-product-compliance
Lightning Source LLC
Chambersburg PA
CBHW071125210326
41519CB00020B/6421